Thank you!

BELMONT COUNTY DISTRICT LIBRARY
Purchased with funds from the
November 2013 Library Levy

ANIMAL SAFARI

Jackals

by Megan Borgert-Spaniol

BLASTOFF! READERS

BELLWETHER MEDIA • MINNEAPOLIS, MN

Note to Librarians, Teachers, and Parents:

Blastoff! Readers are carefully developed by literacy experts and combine standards-based content with developmentally appropriate text.

Level 1 provides the most support through repetition of high-frequency words, light text, predictable sentence patterns, and strong visual support.

Level 2 offers early readers a bit more challenge through varied simple sentences, increased text load, and less repetition of high-frequency words.

Level 3 advances early-fluent readers toward fluency through increased text and concept load, less reliance on visuals, longer sentences, and more literary language.

Level 4 builds reading stamina by providing more text per page, increased use of punctuation, greater variation in sentence patterns, and increasingly challenging vocabulary.

Level 5 encourages children to move from "learning to read" to "reading to learn" by providing even more text, varied writing styles, and less familiar topics.

Whichever book is right for your reader, Blastoff! Readers are the perfect books to build confidence and encourage a love of reading that will last a lifetime!

This edition first published in 2014 by Bellwether Media, Inc.

No part of this publication may be reproduced in whole or in part without written permission of the publisher. For information regarding permission, write to Bellwether Media, Inc., Attention: Permissions Department, 5357 Penn Avenue South, Minneapolis, MN 55419.

Library of Congress Cataloging-in-Publication Data

Borgert-Spaniol, Megan, 1989-
Jackals / by Megan Borgert-Spaniol.
   p. cm. – (Blastoff! readers. Animal safari)
 Summary: "Developed by literacy experts for students in kindergarten through grade three, this book introduces jackals to young readers through leveled text and related photos"– Provided by publisher.
 Audience: K to grade 3.
 Includes bibliographical references and index.
 ISBN 978-1-60014-910-8 (hardcover : alk. paper)
 1. Jackals–Juvenile literature. I. Title. II. Series: Blastoff! readers. 1, Animal safari.
 QL737.C2B67 2014
 599.77'2–dc23
                                                             2013000884

Contents

What Are Jackals?

Jackals are **mammals** with large, pointed ears. They belong to the dog family.

Most jackals live
in dry grasslands.
Some make their
homes in forests
or **marshes**.

Eating

Jackals feed on **insects**, snakes, and birds. They also eat plants and fruits.

Sometimes jackals
work together
to hunt small
antelopes.

Jackals often **scavenge**. They search for dead animals to eat.

Jackals also **steal** their dinner. They follow cheetahs or hyenas on the hunt.

They **howl** to tell others when they find food.

Jackal Family

Female jackals give birth to several **pups**. They raise the pups in holes called **dens**.

den

Adults in a **pack** protect the pups. They fight animals that come on their land. Get away!

Glossary

dens—places where animals rest or raise their young

howl—to let out a long, loud cry

insects—small animals with six legs and hard outer bodies; insect bodies are divided into three parts.

mammals—warm-blooded animals that have backbones and feed their young milk

marshes—wetlands with grasses and other plants

pack—a group of jackals

pups—baby jackals

scavenge—to feed on the meat of a dead animal

steal—to take from another

To Learn More

AT THE LIBRARY
Gibbs, Maddie. *Jackals*. New York, N.Y.: PowerKids Press, 2011.

Markle, Sandra. *Jackals*. Minneapolis, Minn.: Lerner Publications, 2005.

Sapre, Reshma. *The Traveller, the Tiger, and the Very Clever Jackal*. Ocean, N.J.: Grantha Corporation, 2010.

ON THE WEB
Learning more about jackals is as easy as 1, 2, 3.

1. Go to www.factsurfer.com.

2. Enter "jackals" into the search box.

3. Click the "Surf" button and you will see a list of related Web sites.

With factsurfer.com, finding more information is just a click away.

Index